D1519321

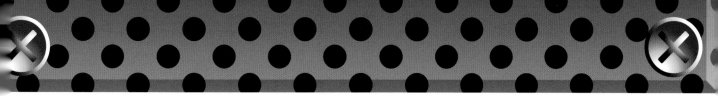

Science in My World: Level 2

MAGNETS

Christian Lopetz

A Crabtree Seedlings Book

CRABTREE
Publishing Company
www.crabtreebooks.com

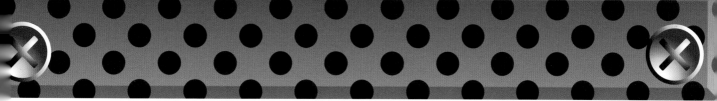

Table of Contents

Magnets

A magnet is something that **attracts** certain kinds of metal.

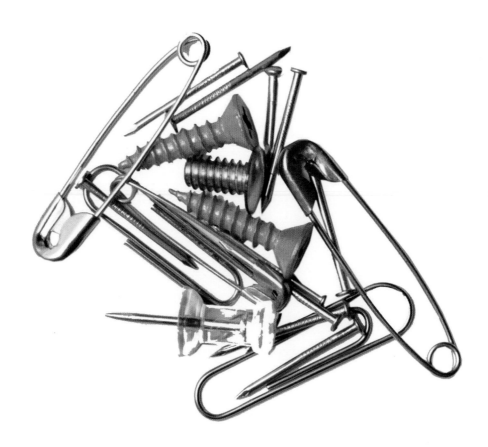

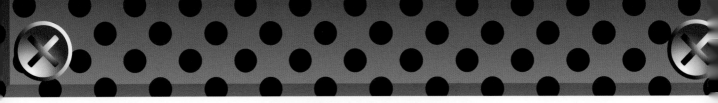

When a magnet attracts a metal object, it pulls the object close and sticks to it.

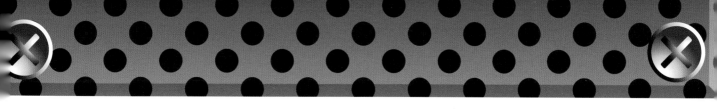

If a magnet sticks to a metal object, we say that object is **magnetic**.

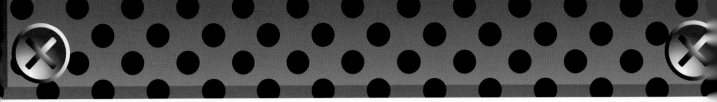

Magnets do not stick to plastic, glass, or wood. Plastic, glass, and wood are not magnetic.

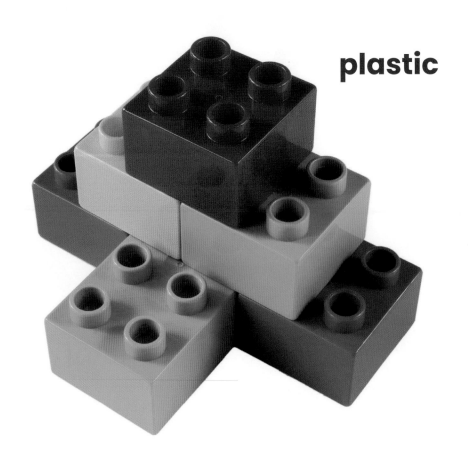

plastic

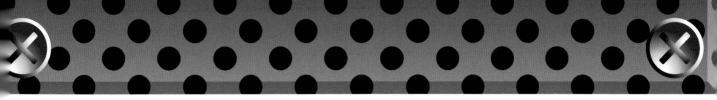

glass

wood

All magnets have a **magnetic field**. This is the area around the magnet that attracts magnetic objects.

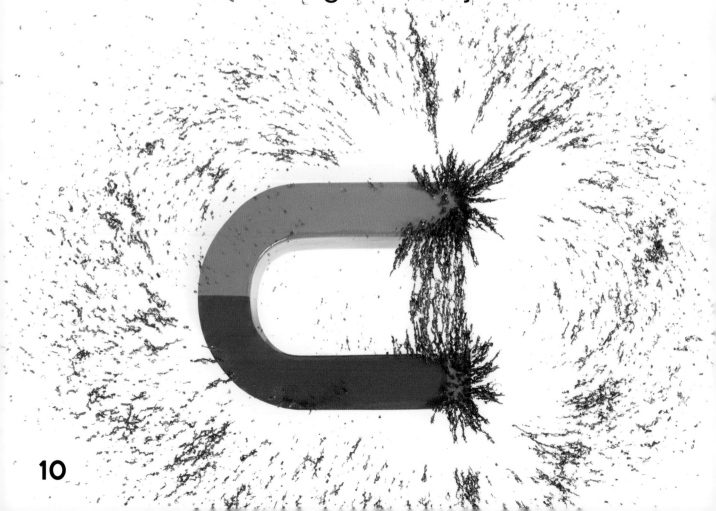

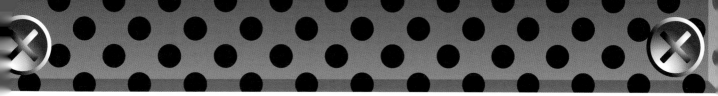

We cannot see magnetic fields.

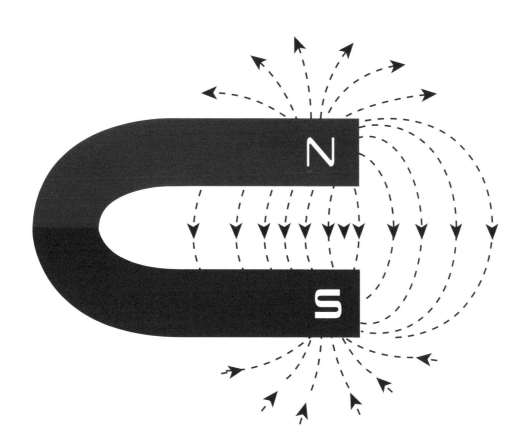

Which of these objects are magnetic?

glass bottle

scissors

plastic bottle

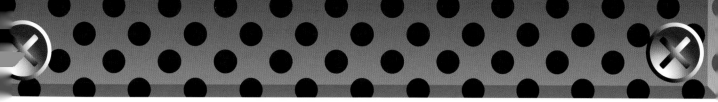

spoon

nuts and bolts

dice

13

Magnets come in many shapes and sizes. Some magnets are shaped like horseshoes.

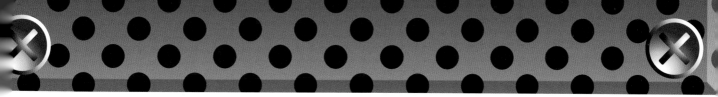

Others are shaped like circles or bars.

Magnetic Poles

Magnets are strongest at their ends. These ends are called the north **pole** and south pole.

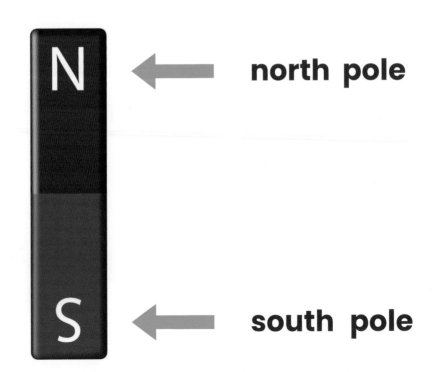

north pole

south pole

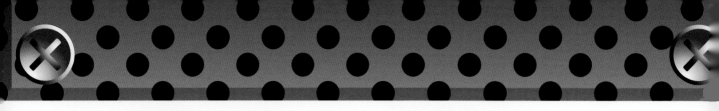

Opposite poles attract each other. They pull together!

Like poles **repel** each other. They push each other away.

S   N

N   S

19

Earth is magnetic. Using a **compass** we can tell which way is north.

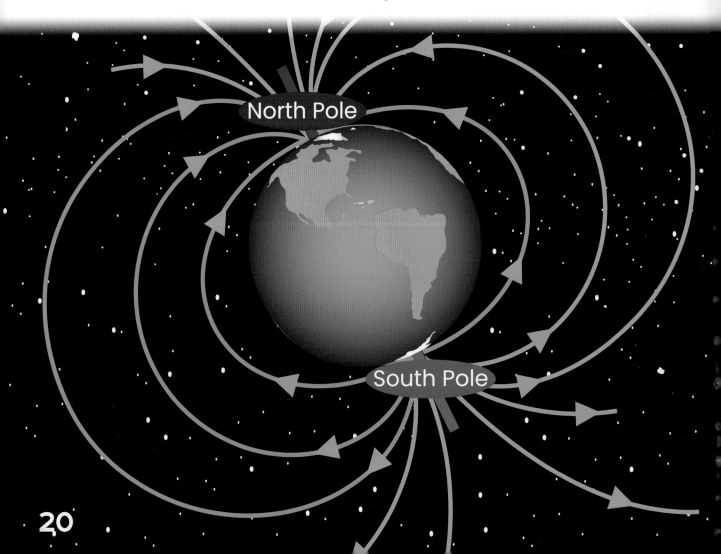

North Pole

South Pole

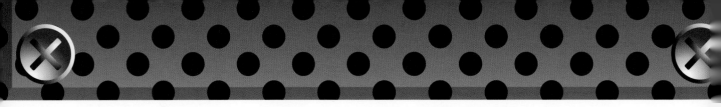

A compass needle is magnetic and always points north.

Earth's North Pole attracts the needle.

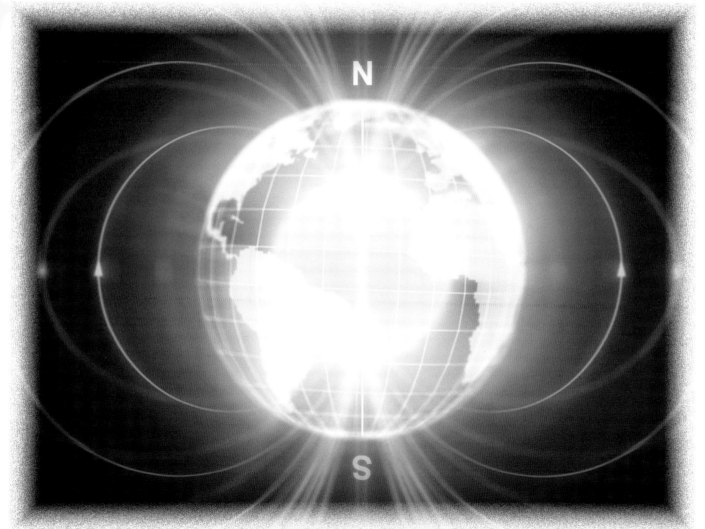

Magnet Power

We use magnets to hold things and to pick things up.

Some magnets are stronger than others!

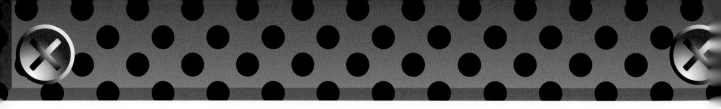

We use magnets inside many machines. There are magnets inside computers and electric toothbrushes.

26

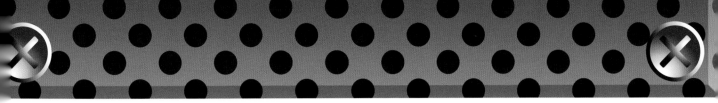

Hospitals use powerful magnets to look inside our bodies.

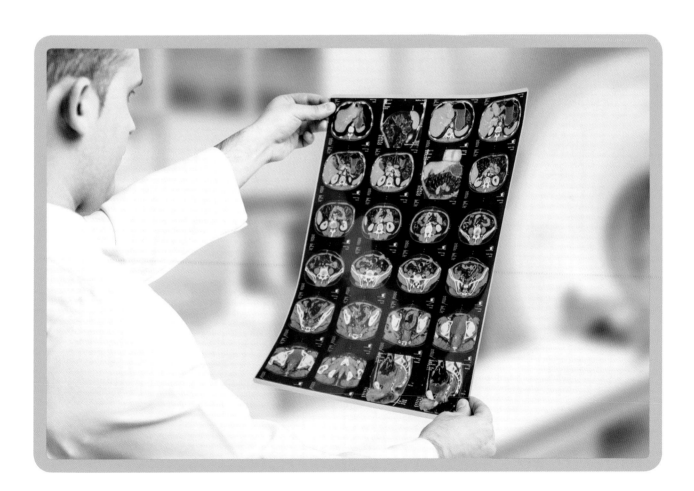

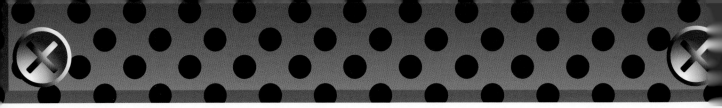

Glossary

attracts (uh-TRAKTS): Pulls close

compass (KUHM-puhss): A tool used to find directions that has a magnetic needle that always points north

like (LIKE): The same

magnetic (MAG-neh-tik): Attracted to magnets or magnetic fields

magnetic field (MAG-neh-tik FEELD): The area around a magnet that attracts certain metals

opposite (OP-uh-sit): Completely different

pole (POHL): The end of a magnet where the pull is strongest

repel (ri-PEL): To push away

Index

School-to-Home Support for Caregivers and Teachers

This book helps children grow by letting them practice reading. Here are a few guiding questions to help the reader build his or her comprehension skills. Possible answers appear here in red.

Before Reading

- **What do I think this book is about?** *I think this book is about magnets that can be used as toys. I think this book is about how magnets can help us in our world.*

- **What do I want to learn about this topic?** *I want to learn where we find magnets. I want to learn some useful things that magnets can do.*

During Reading

- **I wonder why...** *I wonder why a magnet has a north pole and a south pole. I wonder why a compass needle always points north.*

- **What have I learned so far?** *I have learned that magnets are strongest at their ends. I have learned that Earth is magnetic.*

After Reading

- **What details did I learn about this topic?** *I have learned that there are magnets in many machines, such as computers. I have learned that hospitals use magnets to look inside our bodies.*

- **Read the book again and look for the glossary words.** *I see the word **magnetic** on page 7, and the word **compass** on page 20. The other glossary words are found on page 30.*

Library and Archives Canada Cataloguing in Publication

Title: Magnets / Christian Lopetz.
Names: Lopetz, Christian, author.
Description: Series statement: Science in my world: level 2 | "A Crabtree seedlings book". | Includes index.
Identifiers: Canadiana (print) 20210206446 |
    Canadiana (ebook) 20210206454 |
    ISBN 9781039600393 (hardcover) |
    ISBN 9781039600461 (softcover) |
    ISBN 9781039600539 (HTML) |
    ISBN 9781039600607 (EPUB) |
    ISBN 9781039600676 (read-along ebook)
Subjects: LCSH: Magnets—Juvenile literature. |
    LCSH: Magnetism—Juvenile literature.
Classification: LCC QC757.5 .L66 2022 | DDC j538/.4—dc23

Library of Congress Cataloging-in-Publication Data

Available at the Library of Congress

Crabtree Publishing Company
www.crabtreebooks.com   1–800–387–7650

Written by Christian Lopetz
Print coordinator: Katherine Berti

Print book version produced jointly with Blue Door Education in 2022

Printed in the U.S.A./062021/CG20210401

Content produced and published by Blue Door Publishing LLC dba Blue Door Education, Melbourne Beach FL USA. Copyright Blue Door Publishing LLC. All rights reserved. No part of this book may be reproduced or utilized in any form or by any means, electronic or mechanical including photocopying, recording, or by any information storage and retrieval system without permission in writing from the publisher.

Photo Credits: Cover ©shutterstock.com/Marcel Mooij, Page 4/5 ©Blue Door Publishing. Page 2/3 ©shutterstock.com/ New Africa. Page 4/5 ©shutterstock.com/Show all, BlueDoorPublishing. Page 6/7 ©shutterstock.com/Bo Valentino, Rorodaev, knotsmaster, Tatiana Popova, Morgan Lane PhotographyPage 8/9 ©shutterstock.com/Winbjork, By Lipskiy, Nakic, Sandra van der Steen. Page 10/11 ©shutterstock.com/Milan. ©shutterstock.com/Jakinnboaz, Page 12/13 ©shutterstock.com/Matthew Cole, ©shutterstock.com/ Handatko. Page 14/15 ©shutterstock. com/ revers, ©shutterstock.com/ilona.shorokhova. Page 16/17 ©shutterstock.comMatthew Cole. Page 18/19 ©shutterstock.com/Alex Staroseltsev, Yellow Cat. Page 20/21 ©shutterstock.com/Snowbelle, ©shutterstock.com/Casimer. Page 22/23 ©shutterstock.com/John Stebbins, ©shutterstock.com/ Andrey VP. Page 24/25 ©shutterstock.com/Valdecasas, ©shutterstock.com/dvande. Page 26/27 ©shutterstock.com/John Stebbins, ©shutterstock.com/Chinnapong. Page 28/29 ©shutterstock.com/ KaliAntye. ©shutterstock.com/Roman Zaiets

Published in the United States
Crabtree Publishing
347 Fifth Ave.
Suite 1402-145
New York, NY 10016

Published in Canada
Crabtree Publishing
616 Welland Ave.
St. Catharines, Ontario
L2M 5V6